Birds on a Wire

Karen Stubbs is the founder and leader of Birds on a Wire, a ministry designed to equip moms through truth, encouragement and community. Karen is the wife of Greg Stubbs, they have four children, Kelsey, Emily, Taylor and Abby and reside in Cumming, Ga.

After graduating from Auburn University, she and Greg moved to Virginia Beach where Greg served in the Navy as a fighter pilot. The Navy was where Karen gained her passion for motherhood and grew in her reliance on God to get her through the tough Navy years as a young mom. She is passionate about challenging moms to experience motherhood in the way God intended it for them and their families.

THIS BOOK BELONGS TO:

....

....

80 Tips On Motherhood

Cover designed by Christian Art Gifts

Images used under license from Shutterstock.com

© 2017 by Christian Art Gifts

Copyright © in published edition Christian Art Gifts
Copyright © in devotions Karen Stubbs

ISBN 978-1-4321-1962-1

Printed in China

– 80 TIPS ON –
Motherhood

Karen Stubbs

CONTENTS

CONTENTS

FOREWORD

Once upon a time I was a young mom with three small kids at home and little idea what I was doing. That was over twenty years ago, but I remember those days like yesterday. How was I supposed to care for my kids well and maintain a healthy marriage at the same time? I mean, it was a LOT. What did it look like to prioritize my time in this season of life? And that pesky dinner thing relentlessly rolled around every day!

Being a new mom feels much like fumbling through the dark, trying to figure out life with a needy little sidekick. I remember telling my dad, "This is the most CONSTANT thing I've ever done!" I often think how nice it would have been to have a mentor like Karen Stubbs in my life during that season—someone who'd been through it all before and could help me navigate the rough waters of motherhood.

Whenever I read something from Karen, I can't help but nod along, agreeing with the biblical wisdom and practical nuggets she shares. 80 Tips on Motherhood is another wonderful read, a perfect balance of the no-nonsense advice and heartfelt encouragement I've come to expect from Karen.

This book is an absolute treat—like having Karen right by your side, encouraging you that you can do this important job well and shining her light to help you find your way.

Sandra Stanley

TAMING TECHNOLOGY - OR -
THRIVING IN THE WORLD OF TECHNOLOGY

Moms, let's be real: we have a love/hate relationship with technology. We love it when our child is being entertained, but we hate it when our child cannot function without it–or when they think they cannot function without it. As moms, this is a time when we need to step up and put limits on technology.

Here are my tips for taming technology in your family:

- Limit the amount of screen time. Whether it's playing games on your phone or looking though Instagram/Snapchat photos, we all need limits on the amount of time we are using technology. It's not that technology is evil (it's not), but it is a time waster. Set a time that is appropriate for your child and stick with it. It's the same principle as when our parents used to turn off the TV and say, "Go outside and play."

- No technology at the dinner table. Family dinners should consist of gathering around the table and talking to one another, looking people in the eyes, and having a real conversation. You cannot engage with someone if you are looking at your phone. Instead of being on your phones at dinner, here's a thought: talk to each other. Ask your child what was the best and worst thing about their day. Engage with your child by listening to their point of view.

- Put the charging station for all technology in your master bedroom at night. Our minds need a break. It is a good idea to put the phones to bed at night so our children can actually sleep soundly.

Now, moms, in order for these three easy steps to work, you MUST stick with the program. Don't give in to your child's reasoning. Keep telling yourself, "I'm the mom, I know what is best."

Technology is fine in moderation. It only becomes a problem when we allow it to take over our lives. As the mom, you are the gatekeeper.

REFLECTIONS

VACATION MINDSET

Here are a few tips that may help you as you prepare for a few days away with your loved ones this summer:

- Light as a feather. Keep your packing as simple as possible. Lighter is better. Many places where you vacation will have a washer/dryer available, so you don't have to pack your whole closet. Besides, everything you pack needs to be unpacked at one point or another, and in some places you will be hauling it up and down stairs.

- Bigger is not always better; keep it simple. We always think of grand places to visit and awesome things to do so we can post on Instagram. But often, especially when you have little ones, simple is best. With two little ones on our recent trip, we kept it very simple. Every day we carved out times for naps to keep the children on their regular schedules, and most days all we did was hang out at the beach or pool. That was it, and believe me, that was plenty. Being at the beach with a two-and-a-half-year-old and an eight-month-old is a lot of work. The main reason for this vacation was for our family to be together, and that is exactly what we did!

- Make simple memories. At the end of our vacation, I went around the room and asked everyone what their favorite part of the vacation was. The list included golf cart rides, feeding the wild deer on the island, watching the vacation through a child's eyes, games with the family, and just being together. Isn't that something—none of those things involved a lot of money or fanfare!

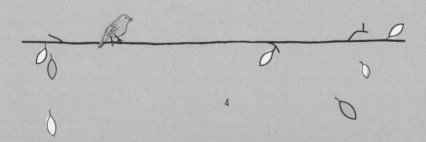

REFLECTIONS

_____
_____
_____
_____
_____
_____
_____
_____
_____
_____
_____
_____
_____
_____
_____
_____
_____
_____
_____
_____
_____

⤳ VACATION ⤳

Vacations can be wonderful, but they can also be very stressful and extremely expensive. Something happens on vacation . . . we become delusional, thinking that the calories we eat and the money we spend on vacation do not count.

One year, Greg and I decided to take all the kids to Disney World. It is a magical place, but it can also be a magically expensive place for a family of six! Greg and I decided early on that we wanted to save up our money so the vacation would be paid for before we even left. We then sat down with all of our children and told them that we were going to pay for the transportation, hotel, three meals a day, and one souvenir for each child, but anything beyond that our children had to pay for themselves. If Kelsey or Emily wanted an ice cream, they would be buying it themselves.

Honestly, it ended up being the best vacation we ever had. I loved it because I wasn't telling my children "no" all day long. When they asked for ice cream, I would say, "sure, buy it if you have the money." Then I would let them decide what they wanted to do. It did not take the children long to realize that these items add up quickly. You may be surprised at how mature your children can be when the decision is on them. When a child has to pay $7 for an ice cream cone, they start to not want it as badly.

REFLECTIONS

WITCHING HOURS

What is the witching hour? It's that time in the late afternoon or early evening when your children seem to lose all control and everyone is getting on each other's nerves. It's also the time of day when your husband is stuck in traffic, and you are texting him every 10 minutes to ask, "WHEN are you going to be home?"

What can we do during these witching hours?

- Try to work on dinner earlier in the day so you only have to pop something in the oven or place it on the grill.
- Save a "good" activity for the kids during this time of the day. As moms, we have usually exhausted our bag of tricks by 4:00 in the afternoon. Instead, reserve at least one or two tricks.
- If your children cannot seem to keep their hands to themselves and continue to aggravate their siblings, it's okay to separate them. It's better to separate and put everyone in their own corners than have mutiny.
- Try what I used to do and throw everyone outside until dinner time. Tell them to find something to do that uses their imaginations.
- Save the favorite TV show for the last resort. If it reaches 5:00pm and dad is still 45 minutes out, use the TV show to entertain them until dinner.
- Lastly, give yourself a break. You don't have to put a five-course gourmet meal on the table each night. Crock-pots can be your best friend during this stage of life.
- Don't forget to breathe!

REFLECTIONS

CHRISTMAS SURVIVAL GUIDE

This Tip On Motherhood more than likely finds you wrapping up all of your holiday errands, preparing for out-of-town guests, or packing your bags to travel to see family. Whether you are traveling, staying home, buying last-minute stocking stuffers, or actually home doing something wonderful like baking cookies with the children, I want to wish you and yours a very Merry Christmas.

At my house, the family has arrived and the house is full of noise again, which this mother of four loves. I know there will be moments of laughter and good memories will be made, but I also know that with all the different personalities in the house, there might be frustration and a few tears shed as people adjust their "normal" to accommodate others.

As the mom, I need to set the pace and try to be as flexible as possible. I've experienced enough Christmases to know that the more flexible I am, the better time I will have. I have to realize that life rarely goes as planned, and what I have in my mind doesn't always happen.

Christmas is a time to gather with loved ones and friends and remember a very special birthday – Christ our Lord's. In Luke we see how Mary the mother of Jesus handled things when life did not turn out the way she had planned. After all, she found herself pregnant before marriage and gave birth to Jesus in a stable, surrounded by animals and shepherds. I think we can all learn from Mary in how she responded to these circumstances. Luke 2:19 says, "But Mary treasured up all these things and pondered them in her heart." I pray that you will be able to treasure the time as well.

REFLECTIONS

HOW TRADITIONS ARE BORN

Christmas pressure!!! Good grief, sometimes I, as a mom, cannot even take it. How in the world can we create Hallmark moments in our homes throughout the Christmas season?

When I think back over my life as a mom, the thing that strikes me the most is that what I wanted to become a great memory for my children usually ended up being a thorn in their side, and what I never intended to make the "great memory" list is what my children remember the most.

For instance, one Christmas my mom told me that she was changing the Christmas lunch to a slightly later time. That year I made breakfast for my family with homemade biscuits, country ham, and eggs. My reasoning was very practical: fill up the bellies of the children, and when 1:00pm rolls around they won't be so grouchy. I never intended to start a Christmas tradition, but a tradition was born that Christmas morning. The next year, my children asked if I was going to make the same breakfast as last year. I told them I wasn't planning to. Almost in unison my children replied, "Mom, we ALWAYS have that breakfast, it's tradition." So a new tradition was born. Now, every Christmas morning I make homemade biscuits, country ham, and eggs.

The point of my story is: relax! Traditions will be born in your family, but don't try to force them. Traditions start because people want to repeat what feels good. Your "feel good" moment in your house will probably be very different than mine, and that is what makes it special to YOUR family. Ask your children, what is one thing that you think about when you think of Christmas (besides gifts)? Whatever their answer is, that is probably the tradition that is forming in your home.

REFLECTIONS

DEFINING EXPECTATIONS

Expectations can be as simple as, "I expect my husband to take out the trash." Webster's Dictionary says expectation is "a belief that something will happen or is likely to happen." In marriage or in parenting, we, as moms, take on certain beliefs as to what we believe WILL happen. Let's use our "trash" example. If your belief is that your husband will take out the trash, and then he doesn't do it, it is highly likely that you will get angry at your husband because your mindset will be, "It was his job."

The problem with expectations is that they put us in a debt/debtor relationship. We begin to adopt the mind-set that certain things are "owed" to us. In a marriage or in a parenting role, it is not wise to get into this type of pattern. Disappointment and anger are usually close behind. Our husbands and children do not "owe" us anything.

Now, it is okay to have desires. I desire for my husband to take out the trash. But expecting my husband to take out the trash all the time will change the dynamic of our relationship to a debt/debtor relationship.

Practice makes perfect. You may have to apologize to your husband and acknowledge that you have had lots of expectations about what you want him to do or say. I'm sure he would love to hear that you are going to work very hard on not placing those expectations on him in the future. If you are very brave, you can ask your husband to gently remind you about your new way of life if he feels you are slipping back into your old habits. (The key word is "gently.")

OUR HUSBANDS & CHILDREN DO NOT "OWE" US ANYTHING.

REFLECTIONS

FAMILIES ARE A BLESSING

"Most of all, love each other as if your life depended on it. Love makes up for practically anything." –1 Peter 4:8, MSG

I love family, don't you? I love my family of six; I love watching my children grow. I love my extended family, both my side and Greg's side. I love how our families interact and how there is laughter, joy, and a ton of fun. Families are a blessing. Do we really comprehend that to the fullest?

There are many things that grow and build a happy marriage. One of the most important things I have learned over the last 26 years is that I need to love and accept Greg for the way he is, and not try to change him to be more like me! I know that sounds like a simple concept, but it has taken me a LONG time to really get it. The same principle is true with our family. A big reason that families fight and argue is because family members don't accept one another the way they are. Instead, they are constantly trying to change each other. Not accepting someone the way they are brings strife. Both people end up frustrated – the person trying to change someone else, and the person being forced to change.

We all need to relax and enjoy one another! If we were all alike, life would not be fun! Enjoy the different personalities represented in your family and learn to appreciate people who are different from you. Embrace the crazy side of others. If you accept others for who they are, they will want to be around you . . . and your "family time" will be full of "quality time" together.

Embrace the *crazy side* of others

REFLECTIONS

HOW DO I STOP RESENTING MY HUSBAND

My tip on not resenting your husband is this: Don't get STUCK in the yuck!

I think word pictures help explain a situation better than a bunch of words. For my word picture on marriage, I think about American pioneers traveling from the east coast to California. These people had a hard journey ahead of them. The terrain was rough, the weather was almost unbearable at times, and sometimes they had to travel through dangerous Indian territory. I think it is hard for us to even comprehend the magnitude of this journey. But the pioneers had a dream of a better life, and they were willing to brave all the hardships to get to that life.

Marriage is the same way. The day you say, "I do," you start your journey together. Marriage has rough terrain, and sometimes our wagon wheel can get stuck in mud. I think the key to a successful marriage is to keep moving. Don't allow your wagon wheel to get stuck in the yuck – do what you need to do to get unstuck and keep plowing ahead.

Here are a few suggestions to help the resentment melt away:

1 - Have conversations with your husband. Tell him the areas where you are frustrated and figure out some solutions together.
2 - Take your concerns to God and ask him to fill in the gaps. Remind yourself of your husband's great qualities. If you can't find any, ask God to reveal to you the things he loves about your husband.
3 - Realize that the journey of marriage is hard, and there will be challenges along the way, but try not to take it out on the one person whom you've chosen to take the journey with.

REFLECTIONS

NAGGING WIFE

"A quarrelsome wife is like the constant dripping of a leaky roof." –*Proverbs 19:13*

No one wants to be the wife who nags, but we are all guilty of it at times. It takes determination and constant submission to God to steer clear of this trap. We quarrel and fight with our husbands because we want our way. We want our husbands to clean the house, to watch the children, to be the spiritual leader, to provide financially for our family, to go the extra mile in the marriage. When these things don't happen, we start to fight or nag, like a constant dripping faucet. A dripping faucet is not effective, it is just annoying. We don't want to be that wife who is constantly complaining, the wife whose husband never hears her because he begins to tune out her voice.

So, then, what do we do with all of our complaining? Do we just forget about it? Push it under the rug and hope that our husband will wake from his slumber one day and correct his ways? We must start taking our complaints, our needs, and our desires to God. Lay your burdens at His feet and ask Him to meet your needs. Allow God to meet you where you are and take that burden off of your husband. God did not create your husband to be your everything – that is God's job. Sometimes God uses your husband to meet your needs, but that is just a bonus! Only God can meet all of your needs and satisfy you completely, so start looking to Him.

Lay your burdens at HIS FEET & ASK HIM to meet your needs

REFLECTIONS

TIPS TO STAY CONNECTED TO YOUR HUSBAND

Helpful tips to keep your husband front and center in your life.

- Carve out 10 minutes a day to debrief each other's day. This activity saved my sanity when the children were little. I needed those ten minutes! During those few minutes I would tell him about my day and he would do the same. I shared with him the highs and the lows of my day and asked him how his day went. After those 10 minutes, I was good.

- Date nights are a must in a marriage. I'm not sure why, but it is hard to date your spouse. I guess in the back of our minds we feel like we have them, so what's the point? The point is … we want to keep them! Deciding what to do on a date is as hard as figuring out when to go. Sit down with your husband and write down several things you like to do. Even write down things you like and your husband likes. Put all these ideas into a jar for date night ideas, and when it's time, pick one.

- I also think it's a good idea to get away with your spouse overnight at least once a year. You need at least three nights away because it usually takes one or two nights for you, as a mom, to finally relax.

- Your marriage is like exercise. If you don't exercise your body and take care of it, you eventually lose your girly figure. Same thing with marriage – you must pay attention to your husband or the flame will eventually go out. Of course, some seasons are harder than others, but after the hard seasons you should for sure give your marriage some extra TLC (Tender Loving Care).

REFLECTIONS

UNREALISTIC EXPECTATIONS

Let's talk about the unrealistic expectations we place on our husbands, children, and families. We are ALL guilty of "dreaming" of how we think life should be. But most of us live life somewhere in between our dreams and reality. The problem comes when we have unrealistic expectations that reality will match our ideals.

What are unrealistic expectations? What does that look like in the "real world?"

- It is unrealistic to think your husband should come home with flowers and candy on a regular basis.
- It is unrealistic to think your child will never make a mistake.
- It is unrealistic to think your children will not fuss and fight with their siblings.
- It is unrealistic to think your husband is going to clean your house the way you clean your house OR watch your children to the same level that you watch your children.
- It is unrealistic to think you and your husband will always see eye-to-eye about money.
- It is unrealistic to think your child will never be disrespectful or roll their eyes at you.

If you have been married for more than three years, then your husband probably doesn't write you love letters every day, but that doesn't mean he doesn't love you. So many times I place unrealistic expectations on my husband, and I get my feelings hurt when my expectations aren't met. So what if he didn't walk into our home and grab me for a kiss like they do in the movies? Let's get real, the movies are NOT like the real world.

We live in a broken world, so why should we expect our families to be picture-perfect? Let's all give ourselves and the family members who live with us a break. I think everyone would enjoy life a lot more!

REFLECTIONS

⤳ HIT PAUSE ⤳

Being a mom means we are busy. We are constantly working, serving, organizing, planning, and thinking. But sometimes we need to slow down and let the busy world keep going while we hit pause. This exercise is hard to do. When you do slow down or pause, you may be tempted to think that you are being lazy or unproductive. However, sometimes you need to hit the pause button.

What does hitting pause look like for you as a mom? Sometimes you need to pause and just sit quietly before the Lord. Walk outside your door and observe something in nature that you take for granted and never even notice, like ants building their home. Other days when you hit pause, you could sit down with your children when they come home from school and just listen to what they have to say about their day. At night when your children are going to bed, climb into bed with them and ask them how their day was. Don't interrupt them, don't try and make a teaching moment out of what they are telling you, but just listen. Other times you may need to hit pause and spend time with your husband, just the two of you. Take a walk around the block and hold hands.

It's crazy that these simple exercises seem bizarre to us, almost childlike. But, hitting the pause button in life can be very life-giving. Try it today. Pause one time and see what happens. You just might be surprised by the result.

Sometimes we need to
slow down
& let the busy world keep
going while we hit pause

REFLECTIONS

THREE WAYS TO STOP COMPARING

Have you ever found yourself wondering how you compare to another mom or to a friend you haven't seen in a while? The comparison game is REAL! It is also a no-win situation. One of two things happens when you compare: either you feel you are better than the other person, or you feel you are less than the other person. Both situations are destructive, and both damage your heart and mind. How in the world can we stop this constant game of better or worse?

1 - Get comfortable in your own skin. What I mean is, get comfortable with who you are, embrace yourself, and LOVE yourself. You need to love everything about you – the good, the bad, and the ugly. There is a true beauty in someone who loves and accepts herself.

2 - Work on you. We all know the only person you can change is yourself. So in the comparison game, if I am looking at my life and not thrilled with where I find myself, then I need to do something about it, not just sit in the self-pity that is getting me nowhere. I need to work on my situation and myself.

3 - Celebrate others. Here's the hardest part of all: celebrate others whom you feel have more, look better, or travel through life with ease. Celebrate them! Fake it until you can make it, ladies! Celebration is a choice.

Moms, I hope this TOM helps you. I want the best for you, and the best for you is YOU! Believe that. We all have something to offer to this amazing world we live in.

REFLECTIONS

WHERE IS YOUR PLACE

Today, my Tip on Motherhood is about picking a place in your home that is yours – a place where you can go and seek a bit of quiet from the rest of the house and spend time with the Lord. Why is having "your place" so important? It will become familiar, and you will long to go there for some time to just be with yourself and the Lord.

My place is in my bedroom – in my chair next to the window. Over the years, my children have seen me sitting in my chair, with no TV on, and they've learned not to disturb me during this time. I didn't mean for my children to catch me in the act, but looking back I'm glad they did, because I was teaching them the importance of carving out time in our busy world for God.

Moms, I'm not sure where you are in your life right now. Perhaps a quiet time seems like an impossible star to reach, or maybe you don't really have a desire to spend a few moments with God each day. I do challenge you to at least pick your place today. Whether you sit in it today or in a month or even a year from today, at least pick a spot. That is always the first step. The next step is to just start talking to God. Tell him what is going on in your world. Tell him the desires of your heart, your pain, and your joys. Read a verse or two in his Word.

My prayer is that you will learn to love your place, and each day you will be drawn even closer to your Heavenly Father, who loves you dearly and wants a relationship with you, just the way you are.

REFLECTIONS

WHAT'S FOR DINNER

The three dreaded words I hear from my children are, "What's for dinner?" Some days I just want to scream and say, "I don't know! I am sick of cooking, sick of trying to figure out what we will all eat, and sick of hearing everyone complain that they didn't like what I chose to make." Am I alone, moms? (Please say, "No Karen, you are not alone!")

So today, my Tips on Motherhood is designed to give you lovely ladies some suggestions for dinner. We all need a little help every now and then, so I decided to write out some of my favorite, easy recipes that you can whip up quickly. Now, before we get started, let's get one thing straight: I am not an "all organic, no preservatives" kind of cook. I do the best I can, but if a box of mac n' cheese is more convenient than homemade, I will choose the box. Let's give each other grace on this stuff. You can adjust the recipes to fit your taste.

Gourmet Chicken
This recipe gets its name from the second year I was married. I made it for one of my friends and she said, "This tastes like Gourmet Chicken." The name stuck.

    4 chicken breasts
    1 stick of butter
    1 lemon
    1 package of dry Italian seasoning

Place raw chicken breasts in a Pyrex dish; mix next three ingredients and pour over chicken.
Bake at 350 degrees for 40 min or until golden brown.

I serve this chicken with a box of Rice-a-Roni Fried Rice and a salad.

REFLECTIONS

Slow Cooker Buffalo Chicken Sandwiches
Recipe yields 6 sandwiches

4 skinless, boneless chicken breast halves
1 (17.5 fluid ounce) bottle buffalo wing sauce, divided (such as Frank's Buffalo sauce)
½ of a package of dry ranch salad dressing mix
2 tbsp butter
6 hoagie rolls, split lengthwise (hamburger buns or Hawaiian rolls work too)

Place the chicken breasts into a slow cooker and pour in three quarters of the wing sauce and the ranch dressing mix. Cover and cook on Low for 6 to 7 hours. Once the chicken has cooked, add the butter and shred the meat finely with two forks. Pile the meat onto the hoagie rolls, and splash with the remaining buffalo wing sauce to serve.

Mozzarella Chicken

4 chicken breasts
4 slices mozzarella cheese
1 can cream of chicken Soup
¼ cup white wine

Place chicken breasts in Pyrex dish; place cheese on top of chicken. Mix white wine and soup together and pour over chicken breasts. Place in pre-heated oven at 350 degrees and bake for 40 min or until chicken is done.

I serve this with white rice, salad, green beans, and rolls if Taylor is home. If your family likes extra gravy, use two cans of soup.

NOTES

∽ RECIPES ∽

We are now deep into winter, and if you are like me, you are sick of being indoors and sick of thinking about what to cook all the time. Today for my TOM I thought I'd share with you one of my favorite soup recipes. The best thing about this recipe is that you can play around with it, add ingredients, spice it up or tone it down, and it's always good! My children love this soup, and it is one of our staples in the Stubbs household!

Chicken Tortilla Soup

½ c chopped onion
½ c chopped green peppers (I use red or yellow)
2 cloves minced garlic
1 tbsp vegetable oil
1 (14 ½ oz) can tomatoes
1 small can green chillis
1 c sliced zucchini (you can also add yellow squash)
½ c picante sauce
1 (10 ½ oz) can beef broth
1 (10 ½ oz) can chicken broth
1 (10 ½ oz) can tomato juice
1 ½ c water
1 tsp ground cumin
3-4 c chicken breast, chopped
½ c rice (optional)
Small can of corn (optional)

In a large Dutch oven, saute onions, peppers, and garlic in oil until tender. Add next 9 ingredients, then add chicken. Add rice and/or corn if desired. Bring to a boil, cover, reduce heat, and simmer for 1 hour. Top with tortilla chips, cheese, and slices of avocado.

This soup is instant comfort food! I hope you and your family enjoy this recipe as much as we do. You can throw any of your favorite veggies in it too.

NOTES

UPSIDE-DOWN CAKE

A friend of mine ordered a pineapple upside-down cake the other day for dessert. She asked me if I wanted a bite, and I said, "No. It just feels strange to me to eat something upside down." Then I got to thinking; life sometimes feels a little upside down, doesn't it?

Before I had children, I thought I would be the mom who would discipline with ease, potty train like a champ, cruise through the teen years without any problems, and navigate through the adult years like it was a piece of cake. But the reality is, ALL of that was hard. Life is like an upside-down cake. We falsely think that 90 percent of our life should be easy with 10 percent challenging, but in reality, we have those percentages backward. Movies make it look easy, Instagram and Facebook make it look perfect, but perfect does not exist because no one is perfect.

So, what do we do with our upside-down life? I believe we should enjoy every bite! Realize early on that life is hard, and that's okay. There will be joyful moments and hard moments, so make the most of life when it is easier and lean into God when it proves to be more challenging. So many times when life gets hard with our children, we ask ourselves, "what am I doing wrong?" The truth is, life is hard – that doesn't mean you are doing anything wrong.

Moms, don't despair, you've got this, even when you feel like you are in way over your head. That's actually a good thing, because when you realize you cannot do it alone, you will reach out to Jesus for help. He is ready and waiting to carry you through the journey.

The truth is, *life is hard* – that doesn't mean you are doing anything wrong

REFLECTIONS

BACK TO SCHOOL

As we gear up for back to school, the organizations are gearing up as well – dance classes, fall sports, Boy Scouts, Girl Scouts, etc. As a mom, I always worried that if I didn't allow my child to sign up for everything, then he/she would be missing out. But every single time, our family would find itself overcommitted, and that is not a great place to be. You know the feeling when you are overcommitted – you're stressed, you feel like you are not doing anything well, and there's no extra time to be found.

This year, before all the sign ups take place, sit down with your child and ask, "What is the most important activity you want to participate in for the fall?" After your child has chosen, look at the activity's schedule and see if it will work with your family's schedule. This step is extremely important if you have more than one child.

When we are part of a family, we need to learn that life is a give-and-take, and we must work together to make our family's choices happen. I believe having these conversations on the front end will help reduce the meltdowns in the long run. When you go for school open house and your son wants to sign up for Boy Scouts, remind him that he said he wanted to play fall baseball and that the meeting times conflict.

Looking back, I realize that during these earlier school years, I did not always take the time to do my research. Most of the time I agreed to do way too much. By October, I was a total mess. I am trying to spare you some of that pain so you can enjoy the activities along with your child!

we need to learn that
life is a give-and-take

REFLECTIONS

SENIOR PICTURES

Life has changed since I was a senior in high school. In my day, when it was senior portrait time, there wasn't a photo shoot. We were assigned a time to show up in the school library, given a drape to put over our clothes, the photographer said to smile, and that was it. It was pretty simple.

When Abby came to me and asked to have her senior portraits taken with a professional photographer, you can imagine my response. You may be thinking to yourself, "Good grief, Karen, she is your fourth child, you should be used to this by now." But, in my defense, it has changed even since Kelsey was a senior. Kelsey's pictures were taken with the school photographer from the yearbook, and she went to their studio and took her pictures there.

To say I resisted hiring a photographer would be correct. I told Abby about the good old days and what I did. She did not appreciate my story. I got the "look" that said I must be very old, and she did say, "times have changed, mom."

Cut to the end of the story: Abby did have a photo session, and I realized something important. Abby walked away that day feeling beautiful. Is it ridiculous that her senior portraits were such a big deal? Yes, I think so. But the look on her face at the end was worth it. Maybe it's not so ridiculous for an almost-18-year-old girl to walk away feeling beautiful and special. I'm glad I came around to her idea for her senior portraits. Sometimes it is worth it for our children to see that we get them, we hear them, and we support them.

REFLECTIONS

PERSONALITIES

Raising four children with four different personalities and temperaments has been challenging to say the least. Throughout my years of being a mom, I've learned that I must be a student of my children and "learn" how God has wired each one of them.

I believe that in parenting a child, if you want the best results, you must play to their strengths. We ALL have strengths and weaknesses. Sometimes I focus only on my child's weaknesses and fail to notice their strengths. When Kelsey was little, maybe around four years old, she would go into her playroom and make a total mess. When it was time to clean up, she didn't want any part of it because she wanted to move on to the next "fun" thing to do around the house. Like a lot of moms, I would stand over her, making her pick up every little thing, and I would not allow her to do anything "fun" until the entire room was clean. Neither of us enjoyed this activity very much.

Then I figured out that Kelsey loved words of affirmation. I changed my tactics and started praising her when she picked up her toys. When her dad arrived home, I bragged about what a great job she did and how smart she was for doing it all by herself. From that moment forward, Kelsey was a master at cleaning up the playroom. I had started playing to her strengths instead of focusing on her weaknesses.

As moms, we need to take time to figure each child out – and it does take a lot of time. So many times I am in a hurry and don't take the time to look at the situation and see the root of the problem. Slow down, learn about your child, and play to their strengths.

As moms, we need to take time to
figure each child out

44

REFLECTIONS

....

....

....

....

....

....

....

....

....

....

....

....

....

....

....

....

....

....

....

....

....

SIBLING RIVALRY

What can I do to prevent sibling rivalry?

How should a mom deal with sibling rivalry? Keep in mind, sibling rivalry goes back to the beginning of time, all the way back to Cain and Abel.

The root of sibling rivalry is jealousy, plain and simple. I think it is easier to teach about something once you can identity what that something is. So in the Stubbs household, we named sibling rivalry The Green Monster. "Green," of course, because it depicts jealousy, and "Monster" because that in my opinion is what it is: a monster that wants to tear apart relationships.

When my children would come crying to me, telling me "it's not fair," I would say, "what is on your back?" Their reply would be, "The Green Monster." I would then say, "what do YOU need to do about the Green Monster?" They would reply with a downcast face, "I need to get him off my back." I would say, "That's right, jealousy will tear you up inside and destroy your relationship with your brother/sister. You don't want that, do you?" Then I would encourage them to go do some heart work.

Heart Work for Conquering the Green Monster

- Acknowledge what you are jealous about in the other person
- Ask God to forgive your jealousy
- Celebrate the other person

You can't prevent sibling rivalry. It is part of life because we are all sinful people. But you can teach your child what to do with it and how to move past it. Think how helpful that one lesson will be for your child's entire life!

REFLECTIONS

BREAKING THE SPIRIT OF YOUR CHILD

One of the most popular questions I get asked is "How do you break a child's will and not their spirit?"

This a great question, and one that I used to ponder as well when my children were young. I think a child's spirit is much harder to break than we realize. One indication of this is that they keep disobeying! When our children are toddlers, we feel as if we are constantly getting after them and constantly disciplining them. This is because we are training them to submit to authority. Let's be clear: no one likes to submit to authority, and children are no different. But we need to parent with the end in mind – there will always be authority to submit to, as long as we are alive . . . teachers, bosses, police, etc. When we teach our children to obey us, we are training our children to one day become adults who respect and submit to authority. This is for their own good.

I believe we need to change our vocabulary from "breaking a child's will" to "teaching a child to submit." So the real question is, how can I teach a child to submit? The answer to that question is that you must teach them that you are their authority, and what you say goes. They must learn to obey first and ask questions later. Teaching submission takes time and consistency.

We, as moms, need to realize once and for all that this job is going to be difficult, and we cannot give up. We must push past the fear that we will break our child's spirit and realize that we are helping them in the long run.

Teaching submission takes
TIME and CONSISTENCY

REFLECTIONS

LOVE PAST THE CUTENESS

Let's be honest: don't we all believe that our child is the cutest child on the planet? Your answer is probably, "YES!!!!!", which is as it should be. Now that we are on the same page, let's get down to what this TOM is all about. Ultimately, it is your job as a mom to see past the cuteness, love past the cuteness, and parent past the cuteness. What I mean is that even though you think your child is adorable, smart, and hands down the best child on the planet, you must teach them values. Teach them how to treat others well, how to share, how to not throw food off their plate, how to wait patiently on others, how to put others before themselves, how to tell the truth, how to work hard, and how to be kind and loving. Do any of these values come naturally to any of us? Not really! What does come naturally is to value "me, myself, and I" more than anyone else.

Loving your child past the cuteness requires you to look past their cute outward qualities and teach them what it says in 1 Samuel 16:7: "People look at the outward appearance, but the Lord looks at the heart." True beauty comes from within.

Teaching values is hard, and it takes time . . . lots and lots of time. It feels never-ending and sometimes defeating. To be a teacher of values you must be patient, you must endure and see the "more" in the child than they see in themselves.

Don't give up, moms! You have a BIG job ahead of you. Teaching and guiding children is not for the faint of heart or the lazy. Keep going – you are doing a great job!

REFLECTIONS

❧ MANNERS ❧

Manners and etiquette seem to be getting lost in our culture. As moms, let's start being intentional about bringing manners and etiquette back into our society. We can start one child at a time. I believe there are a few non-negotiables that we should STILL be teaching our kids:

- Look someone in the eye when you are talking to them . . . even if you are shy.
- Be responsible and "own" your piece of the pie. Don't blame others for your mistakes. Take ownership of what you did wrong.
- You as a child are not entitled to anything. You must work hard and earn your spot on the team, in the classroom, or with your friends.
- When you are wearing a bathing suit, wear a cover-up. Don't show the world everything you got! (Especially not on social media!)
- Do a job, ANY job 100 percent. No job is too small.
- When two adults are talking, don't barge in and ask for something. Wait until there is a pause in the conversation and then say, "excuse me."
- When you are at dinner with family or friends, put down the technology and prioritize the relationship in front of you.

I'm certain more could be added to this list, but it's a start. As I look around at the world today and hear stories from moms, I notice that many problems arise from children not understanding or practicing this list. For now, I will get off my soapbox, but I think if we moms started teaching our children these simple habits, our world as a whole would be a better place.

> "Be intentional about teaching
> *manners & etiquette*
> to your kids today."

REFLECTIONS

⚬⟋ RESPECT ⟍⚬

Aretha Franklin said it best: "R-E-S-P-E-C-T, find out what it means to me." As moms, we need to teach our children, starting at age one, that they need to respect their mom and dad. Children can be disrespectful at any age: the toddler trying to kick you while you are changing their diaper, the middle schooler rolling their eyes, or the teenager talking disrespectfully. The majority of the time, a child is disrespectful because they have been allowed to get away with it.

Moms, you are important! Your job is serious, and you should be treated in an appropriate way. I believe that when we stand up for ourselves and teach our children that our job is worthy of respect, it sends an important message.

Teaching respect starts early in a child's life. When you are changing your child's diaper and he or she tries to kick at you, lower your voice and say firmly, "No, sir! Do not kick mommy." As a child grows a little bit older and begins to roll their eyes at you or tell you to shut up, you need to correct them and say, "You don't talk to me that way." If your teenager is constantly talking "at" you, treating you like you are dumber than dirt, maybe you should remind them, "I am a smart person, and I will not be talked to in that manner."

Stand up for yourself and demand the respect that you should have. You don't need to wait until your husband gets home from work to defend yourself – you can do it on your own. You are important! You are an amazing, beautiful woman whom God created, and you are an awesome mom who deserves to be treated well.

> You are an amazing,
> beautiful woman whom God
> created, and you are an
> *awesome mom*

REFLECTIONS

SOS

"Let us not become weary in doing good, for at the proper time we will reap a harvest if we do not give up." –Galatians 6:9

I received an SOS text from a mom. Her two-year-old was not complying with her wishes, and she felt like a bad mom because she was always getting after him. She even wrote, "I feel like an ogre."

I KNOW that this thought plagues most moms. So I want to share with you a few thoughts that may help when you feel like an ogre.

- When we are training our children in the way they should go, this is not the time to be their friend.
- Training up a child is HARD work and does not happen overnight. A child is like us in the fact they do not like being told "no." But unlike us, they cannot reason. Therefore, they throw fits and scream NO at us.
- Try not to get discouraged. You are doing a good job. Hang in there and don't stop just because you feel like what you are doing is not working.
- Keep in mind what your end goal is. If you want a child to obey you when they are 8, 10, 13, and 17, then you must train them to mind you when they are 2 and 3. You must put in the time in order to get the long-term results you hope to achieve.
- You are not looking for BIG changes, just glimpses that they are hearing you and heeding what you are saying.
- Rejoice when you see a glimpse of improvement. Praise your child. Tell them that you appreciate them obeying you, and that it makes you very happy to see their obedient heart.

REFLECTIONS

A MOTHER'S WORLD

Over the last 26 years, my life as a mom has been stable and steady. While Greg flew F-14s and F-18s, I stayed home and wiped bottoms and noses. The first ten years as a stay-at-home mom were filled with a lot of the same activities – cooking, laundry, nap time, park time, snack time, being outside while the children played, cleaning the house, driving children to practices and doctor's appointments, grocery shopping, dry cleaning trips, and trips to the mall. I've wiped away many tears over the past 26 years, bandaged up lots of boo-boos, and counseled many children dealing with hurt feelings.

After ten years of being a stay-at-home mom I went back to work to give me something to do – because I guess I was nuts! Then I had to learn how to tackle everything I mentioned above and of course be a great employee.

As a mom, I've been exhausted, felt defeated, and wanted to throw in the towel, but even in those moments, God gave me the best reward known to mankind – when my child said, "I love you to the moon and back, Mom." Or when my sweet four-year old put his chubby little fingers on my face and said, "You are so pretty."

What do I want to pass on to the younger generation of moms? Well, I want to tell you that it is all worth it! The sleepless nights, the heartache, the temper tantrums, the fights, the boredom, the loneliness. Hang in there and don't give up. The love you are pouring out is worth it, and you are doing a good job!

THE LOVE
you are pouring out
IS WORTH IT!

REFLECTIONS

A NOTE FROM THE TEACHER

As the big Momma Bird, I've got to tell you that we ALL need to stop being so critical of each other and start giving each other grace.

What am I talking about? I am talking about how critical we are of other moms. From the way we tear each other down, you would think we are on opposing teams or something. But we are all on the same team, desperately trying to do the best we can with what we've been given. You may be a mom who works from 9am to 5pm, and you don't need a stay-at-home mom judging you, saying you don't love your child as much as they do. Or you may be a stay-at-home mom with your master's degree, and you don't need a working mom to patronize you like you don't have a brain in your head. At the end of the day, we are all moms, and we all share the same goal . . . to survive these years of motherhood and come out on the other end semi-sane.

Remember: I love you all! But, if we don't stick together as moms, whom can we turn to? We are ALL on the same team. We live different lifestyles and have different needs, but at the end of the day, do any of us really know what we are doing? NO! I am saying that as a mom of over 26 years. I STILL don't know what I'm doing. But I do know this to be true: I've had great friends stand by me in my hours of despair and just listen to me.

Let's make a pact today – that we are going to be a little more gracious towards our fellow moms and a lot more loving. Wouldn't that be wonderful?

Let's be a little more *gracious* and a lot more *loving* toward our fellow moms today.

REFLECTIONS

APPROVAL

"Am I now trying to win the approval of human beings, or of God?" Galatians 1:10

Do you seek people's approval? What are you after? Are you looking for affirmation that you are doing a good job? Are you searching to find your place in the world, and if you have others' approval then you know you are of worth? Or do you just want people to like you?

I don't think there is anything wrong with trying to please my husband, children, parents, and friends. I believe it all goes wrong when that desire becomes so great that it consumes my life. I want to please my husband, to be a good wife to him, to create a home he wants to come home to, but I can let that get out of control. It is easy for me to be so consumed by wanting to please others that I forget about what God wants.

My ultimate goal should be to win God's approval. If I will focus my time and energy on God and winning his approval, everything else will fall into place. That is because God wants me to love others more than I do myself. He wants me to treat others the way I want to be treated. He wants me to put others first and myself last, to forgive others always, to be kind, loving, and gentle, to have patience and self-control.

If I focus my time on seeking God's approval and doing those things, then I will be a wonderful wife, an awesome mother, a loving child to my parents, and a great friend. I need to start seeking God and looking for Him to say, "well done!"

MY ULTIMATE GOAL SHOULD BE TO WIN GOD'S APPROVAL.

REFLECTIONS

❧BOUNDARIES❧

Today's TOM is how to set up loving boundaries that protect you from unwanted advice from your parents.

My first rule of thumb concerning parents and advice is to let blood deal with blood. If your parents are the ones giving the unwanted advice, it's your job to talk to them. If your in-laws are the ones giving the unwanted advice, have your husband lead the conversation. This is important because "blood" will forgive "blood" quicker than non-blood. As a wife, you want to protect your spouse as much as you can, and he needs to protect you. Secondly, I think it's always best to have these conversations during a neutral time, not in the heat of the moment.

Start the conversation something like this: "Mom and Dad, let me first say that I appreciate everything you do for me and my children. I think you are wonderful parents, and I have learned a lot from you over the years. I would like to talk to you about a problem that keeps occurring, which is when you give me unsolicited advice on my parenting. I know you are trying to help me and are not trying to hurt me in any way. I know you've walked this road before, and you see things from a different perspective than I do. While I appreciate all your wisdom, I start to second guess myself on everything, and that makes me unsure of my decisions. So I would love for you not to give advice unless I specifically ask for it. I want our relationship to stay strong and close, and I believe this will help keep it that way."

REFLECTIONS

❧ BUSY LIFE ❧

"The sun rises and the sun sets, and hurries back to where it rises." –Ecclesiastes 1:5

I ran across this verse the other day, and I am really relating to the "sun" these days. I feel like I go throughout my day, accomplishing everything that needs to get done, and then I hurry to the next day to start it all over again. We live in a BUSY world!!! Rush, rush, rush, is usually my motto and my pace. I have to force myself to slow down, force myself to throttle back on my to-do list.

This past Saturday, I actually sat down, went through recipes, figured out my menu for the week, looked through my pantry to see what I have and don't have, and then I made my grocery list. I then took my time at the grocery store, going up and down each aisle with purpose. When I arrived home with my car full of groceries, I felt like I had accomplished so much that day.

I'm not going to tell you as a mom to cut out all of your activities, to quit your job, or to move out to the country and sit on your front porch and sip lemonade all day long. That is unrealistic. Our culture is much more fast-paced than that. But every now and then it does do a soul good to slow down, take a deep breath, and do our job with purpose.

Think about it: what is one activity you could do with purpose this week?

- clean out your pantry
- change your closet from winter to summer clothes
- make a menu for the week
- clean out the "junk" drawer in your kitchen
- clean out ANY drawer in your kitchen:)

REFLECTIONS

COMBATING FEAR

Today's TOM is about combatting fear. When I saw the topic for this week's podcast on my schedule and started to write, I remembered that combatting fear is so close to my heart that I have written about it frequently: there is a devotional on this topic in my book and we focused an entire Soar conference on it as well.

Fear is a stronghold that the enemy uses against moms to keep us worried, anxious, and apprehensive. But, ladies, we do not need to be fearful. We need to be strong and courageous and know beyond a shadow of a doubt that our God goes before us. He is mighty! If I am fearful as a mom, what am I passing onto my children? Fear, anxiety, and unrest.

Is that the legacy I want to leave with my child? No! I want to be strong, confident, full of peace, and I want my children to be the same. Peace comes from trusting in God.

WE NEED TO BE
STRONG AND COURAGEOUS
& KNOW BEYOND A SHADOW
—— OF A DOUBT THAT ——
OUR GOD GOES BEFORE US

REFLECTIONS

CONFIDENT MOM

Motherhood has the ability to bring the most confident of women to her knees in utter frustration. Motherhood also has the ability to make you feel like the biggest hero on the planet. As a mom, I have felt both sides of this coin. Being a mom is the most rewarding and challenging job I have ever had.

How can I be a confident mom? Let's first define what confidence is. According to the Webster New World Dictionary, confidence is defined as "a firm belief; trust or reliance." The question for every mom is, "Where do you place your trust?" There are many answers to that question, and for me, the answers have changed throughout the years. The things I have trusted to always be the same are my children's health and safety, my husband's career, my ability as a mom, and my support system. I can say that at different times throughout my 26 years of being a mom, my confidence was shaken in each of these areas.

The reason it is important to know where we're placing our trust is because the object of our confidence determines whether or not we are shaken when things don't go according to plan. So many times we assume life will go our way, we will never get sick, our children will always excel, or our world will never be torn apart, but there are no guarantees for any of that.

My challenge to you this week in our TOM is to ask yourself, "Where do I place my confidence?" You may be surprised at your answer.

Where do you place your trust?

REFLECTIONS

~ CONQUERORS ~

In Joshua 1:9, God gives Joshua a bold charge for the Israelites. He says, "Be strong and courageous. Do not be afraid; do not be discouraged, for the Lord your God will be with you wherever you go." Take a minute and just think about that verse. We live in a terrifying world, to be sure. God is telling me not to be afraid or discouraged BECAUSE God will be with me. Ladies, that is an amazing promise. If my husband leaves me and I am a single mom, God will be with me. If my child gets cancer, God will be with me. If lightning strikes my house and I lose all of my earthly possessions, God will be with me.

Think of how it will impact my life to truly believe this verse. I will be able to change the course of my family. I will not be anxious because I know God is with me. I will be able to pass my faith on to my children, because they will see a victorious, bold courageous mom, full of confidence, which in turn will give them confidence.

There is no need to be terrified, because our God goes before us, and even if there is hardship, he will not leave us. You may be thinking, "Good grief, Karen is preaching to us today." I am, I guess, because I want you all to be confident women who place your trust and reliance in the One who is trustworthy. I leave you with Joshua's words again: "Be strong and courageous. Do not be afraid; do not be discouraged, for the Lord your God will be with you wherever you go."

GOD GOES BEFORE US
and even if there is a

hardship

HE WILL NOT LEAVE US

REFLECTIONS

DANCE PARTY!

I was driving home today and heard an old familiar song and turned it up on my radio. A flood of wonderful emotions came rushing through me. When my children were little, I used to have impromptu dance parties in the den to break up the day or at night after bath time to shake things up a bit. We would turn on the music and dance to the music blaring out of the speakers. The girls loved to twirl in their nightgowns, and I remember Taylor just running from one side of the room to the other with a hop at the end. That was his form of dancing, either that or running and bumping into his sisters. Abby would just stand in one position and jump up and down. I'm sure the neighbors wondered what we were doing.

It was so much fun for me and the children, and Greg when he was home. Have you ever done that before? You should try it sometime. Ten or fifteen years later you may be riding down the road and hear a familiar song come on the radio that reminds you of those dance parties, and that same wonderful feeling will come flooding back in your memory. Music is a wonderful outlet of emotions.

Listen, your children don't have to be little, either. Dancing is good at any age. Have a dance party tonight in your home. It doesn't have to be fancy, nothing special, just turn up the music and have fun!

Have a dance party tonight
in your home. It doesn't have to be
fancy, just turn up the music &

have fun!

REFLECTIONS

DO GOODERS

"Therefore, as we have opportunity, let us do good to all people, especially to those who belong to the family of believers" –Galatians 6:10

Doing good sounds like such an easy thing to do. "Of course I'm a good person. Of course I do kind things for people every day," we tell ourselves. And it is true – we do good things for our family and friends all the time. It is natural for us to be kind to those we love.

But Paul challenges us in Galatians to take opportunities to do good for ALL people. "All" people includes strangers at the grocery store, people pumping gas at the gas station, people driving next to me on the highway, my neighbor, and the person on the other end of the line when I call my cell phone carrier because my bill is not right. God gives us opportunities every day to reach out to people and show kindness. I can give the cashier at the grocery store a smile and a greeting instead of staring past her, only thinking of what I'm going to make for dinner. I can let the person coming into my lane of traffic merge . . . and give them a smile.

Little acts of kindness throughout the day add up to "doing good" to the people around you. Be creative. Have you ever paid for a cup of coffee for the car behind you in the drive-through at your local coffee shop? That is a nice gesture, a random act of kindness. Today, go throughout your day thinking, "whom could I bless today?" You might be surprised how much you are blessed by these good deeds and how contagious they will become in your life.

WHOM COULD I
bless today?

REFLECTIONS

FAMILY IS HOME

My daughter Kelsey recently moved to California. It was amazing how quickly the children adapted. Kelsey's children are young, which no doubt made it easier, but what stuck out in my mind was that her children adjusted because Kelsey and Kevin are what makes them feel safe. It's not their toys, their beds, or their stuff that gives them security, but their family. As long as Kevin and Kelsey were close by, Evie and Chapman did great.

Over the years I have stressed and not found contentment because I have wanted material things and been discouraged when I didn't get them. I used to tell myself, "If we had a finished basement, we would be closer as a family. The finished basement would make everything better." In reality, what made my family "better" over the years was not the size of my house, the car I drove, or any other material item. What made my family complete was us all being together and enjoying where we were. One of the best Christmases we ever had was when we lived in a rented house and all of our "stuff" was packed up in storage. We made ornaments out of Play-Doh and a popcorn garland. It was a great season in our lives.

Moms, you may be in a season of contentment or discontentment, but whatever season you are in, I want to challenge you to make the most of where you are and try not to look behind or ahead. Instead of getting caught thinking, "I wish," remember that your children won't remember the material things (or lack thereof), but they will remember the love that filled your home. I think we will all be happier if love is our center instead of the things of this world.

What made my family complete
was us all being together
and enjoying where we were.

REFLECTIONS

FIGHTING IS GOOD

We are told from a very young age not to fight with people. I agree that most of the time fighting is not productive and does not benefit anyone. But there are times when we must fight – and fight hard, until we win. I believe with all my heart that marriage and family are worth fighting for, even though our culture often teaches us to give up. Winston Churchill had some insight on the matter of fighting when he said, "Never give in. Never give in. Never, never, never, never – in nothing, great or small, large or petty – never give in, except to convictions of honor and good sense. Never yield to force. Never yield to the apparently overwhelming might of the enemy."

Churchill was talking about World War II, but what he says applies to marriage and our families as well. Our families are under attack in today's society, and instead of fighting for them, we are giving up and telling ourselves "what is the point?" The point is this: your family is worth fighting for, each and every day! We must fight in order to win this battle that is raging against our families.

The fight must begin in your marriage. Fight to communicate with your husband, fight through those difficult conversations that need to be shared. Don't push your thoughts and feelings down, convincing yourself that one more conversation will not help. Fight to find the love you had for your spouse once again. Fight to keep your husband number one in your life, not to be replaced by the children. Fight when you are tired and weary, fight when you feel like you are doing all the work and he is not even trying. Fight. It is worth the fight.

marriage and family are
worth fighting for

REFLECTIONS

GUILT

What do moms feel guilty about? EVERYTHING! Pick any situation, and I'm pretty confident most moms can figure out a way to feel guilty about it! All this guilt is harming us moms. Guilt holds us back from reaching our full potential. It bogs us down, like we are wading through mud instead of dry land. We are still moving, but we are moving at a slower pace, a more burdensome pace, and we are worn out.

What are we to do? Jesus gives us a great answer. In Matthew 11:28-30, Jesus says, "Come to me, all who are weary and burdened, and I will give you rest. Take my yoke upon you and learn from me, for I am gentle and humble in heart, and you will find rest for your souls. For my yoke is easy and my burden is light."

Do you hear Jesus calling to you? He is. He is saying, "Come to me!" We are weary and we are burdened, but Jesus promises to give us rest if we come to Him. We also play a part in finding rest. We must yoke ourselves to Jesus, which means we must walk life with Him, sharing our burdens and our troubles, and start to do life with Jesus instead of on our own. A yoke is a device used to join two animals, usually oxen, so they can plow a field together. Farmers will pair a seasoned ox with a younger, less experienced ox, so the younger ox can learn from the veteran ox. We are to join ourselves to Jesus and learn from Him because he knows the path of our life. Jesus wants to "do" life with you and relieve you of your burdens, especially the burden of guilt.

JESUS PROMISES TO
give us rest
IF WE COME TO HIM

REFLECTIONS

∽ HANDS FULL ∽

Moms hear it all the time: "You sure have your hands full." I confess that I have said it to other moms. I don't mean it in a negative way, I'm just honestly acknowledging that a mom's hands are full with little ones or a rebellious teen or even with athletic schedules. The point is, all moms are busy!

Recently, Kelsey visited for an extended stay. We LOVED having her and her children in the house. The joy that children bring cannot be matched. We would constantly talk about how adorable and smart Evie was, and then of course how snuggly and sweet little Chapman was. But, ladies, parenting two children under two is no joke, and it's not for the faint of heart. One day I encouraged Kelsey to go on an outing with her sisters, and I volunteered to watch the little ones. The children were incredibly good, but my hands were full. While Evie and Chapman were taking a nap, I made a pan of brownies. Afterwards I thought, "I'll just sit down for a moment and rest while the brownies bake." My bottom had not hit the sofa before I heard Chapman crying. What came to my mind was, "Oh, I remember these days, and poor Kelsey has just started!"

Moms, your hands are full. But they are full of wonderful and amazing things! You are the teacher, the nurse, the cook, the housekeeper; you are the counselor and the all-time best mom in the world to your children. Keep up the good work and don't get discouraged. Your days are long and HARD, but it is so worth it in the end. Hang in there! You are doing an amazing job.

You are doing an *amazing job.*

REFLECTIONS

HOW TO BALANCE LIFE

- Don't try to make things "fair" all the time. In order to keep balance in your home, realize and accept the hard fact that life is not fair. In the end, it all evens out. For example, some birthdays are bigger than others. If one child is turning 10 and another is turning eight, the 10-year-old will probably have a bigger deal made of their day. Why? I don't know, that's just how it is. But then a few years later the eight-year-old will get their turn to have a 10-year-old birthday.

- As a mom, you should try to make each child feel special, but there are seasons in life when you are all just hanging on. I had one mom email me to say she was pregnant with number four, and her other three were close in age. She was concerned that she was not doing enough for the three children while she was pregnant. Honestly, she's in that stage where all she can do is get through each day, and every child is not getting a lot of one-on-one attention. But this is a good time for her children to learn the important lesson that the world doesn't revolve around them. Part of life is learning to be okay with that concept. Your children will survive!

- Keep in mind that you can't do it all. Something or someone has to give a little. Our world likes to tell us to do it all, and that it can be done, but it can't. You have to make priorities and choose what your focus is in life, especially when it comes to your children. Ask yourself, what are the most important things in your life, the things that you want to give the most energy and attention to? Tough choices have to be made or you will try to do everything and frustrate yourself and your family in the process.

REFLECTIONS

HUMBLE, GENTLE, PEACEFUL

"Be completely humble and gentle; be patient, bearing with one another in love. Make every effort to keep the unity of the Spirit through the bond of peace."
–Ephesians 4:2-3

These verses sound so wonderful and easy . . . until life hits you in the face. It's hard to be completely humble when you're sitting across from someone who is talking about how wonderful, talented, and smart their child is. As they brag about their child being the leader of every sport and club they participate in, am I to be humble and not start a brag fest about my children? Yes!

Be gentle . . . when my husband frustrates me for the 50th time in one day? Be gentle . . . when my child is supposed to take out the trash, but leaves it on the garage floor, the dog gets into it and makes a mess, and then the dog throws up on the carpet because he ate things he shouldn't have eaten? Gentle, really? Is that possible? YES!

Be patient, bearing with one another . . . when I am at the grocery store trying to check out in a hurry so I can pick my kids up from school, and the cashier is new and can't seem to get her act together? Patient and bearing with one another? YES!

"Make every effort to keep the unity of the Spirit through the bond of peace." Do I make EVERY effort to keep unity when holidays roll around and the house is filled with family and in-laws and there are lots of personalities meshing together? Do I help bring unity, or do I add to the tension?

Great questions. Moms, we need God's help to accomplish these verses!

REFLECTIONS

～∘I SURRENDER∘～

"My grace is sufficient for you, for my power is made perfect in weakness."
–2 Corinthians 12:9

This verse is a beautiful thought. When you are reading it in the Bible, it's easy to agree that God's grace is amazing and wonderful, and that it is enough. But when life hits us hard and we are weak, this verse is not so fun to live out. I am here to tell you, though, that I have learned from experience that when I am weak, God shines all the more brightly in my life. There is one key to seeing God's power in our weakness, and that is that we have to surrender to him, accepting our weakness and allowing him to do his work in us.

Accepting our weakness is not a fun thing to do. No one likes the thought of being weak, but each one of us is weak at different times and in different areas of our lives. I might have experienced this truth more than the norm because I have always prided myself on being such a "strong" person. Remember the verse, "pride comes before a fall" (Proverbs 11:2).

My point is, when I surrender to God and His plan for my life, when I throw my hands in the air and say, "I surrender all," that is when God's power is made perfect in my weakness and His grace becomes enough for me. When that moment happens in my life, a peace washes over me that I cannot explain. Even if my circumstances do not change, I am okay because I know my heavenly Father is carrying me through the situation.

Let go and let God take control of your life. Experience His grace, for there is nothing like it in the world.

REFLECTIONS

JUGGLING A BUSY LIFE

We have one thing in common where time is concerned: We ALL have 24 hours in a day and seven days in a week. If you are like me, you play many roles. I am a wife and a mom, and I also run a ministry. If I were ONLY a wife or a mom or only had a job, I could manage my time nicely, but I have to juggle all three parts of my life and still be sane. Can it be done? I think it can.

There is a verse in Ephesians 5:15-16 that says, "Be very careful, then, how you live – not as unwise but as wise, making the most of every opportunity, because the days are evil." This verse shows us that we need to manage our time wisely.

Divide your time into three categories:

- Non-negotiables
- Essentials
- Bonus

Non-negotiables are the things in your life that you 100 percent must carve out time for, regardless of how busy you are.

Essentials are the things in your life that are also very important, like shopping for groceries, cleaning your house, and planning for family dinners, kids' school activities, and holidays.

Bonus – you guessed it – are the things in your life that you don't have to do, but are fun to do.

Moms, use this grid. Ask yourself, what are my non-negotiables? What MUST I include in my calendar to keep my life operating at its best? Keep in mind there are many "good" things tugging on you, but you have to pick what is best for your calendar and your life. Be selective. If you are in a hectic season, some of your "good" activities will need to bump down to the bonus category because there is no margin for them.

REFLECTIONS

JUST DO IT!

I recently remembered a time when thunderstorms and tornadoes were on their way to Georgia. With storms looming, what do you think my first thought was as a wife and mom? I need to get to the grocery store before the rain comes!

What is looming in your life right now?

- Do you need to tackle that stack of bills and finally get your credit card paid off?
- Do you need to clean out your "junk" drawer? (We all have them!)
- Do you need to talk to your husband about your teenager, whom you think might be going in the wrong direction, but you have been trying to ignore that thought because you don't know what to do?
- Do you need to slow your life down because you are in hyper warp speed and if something doesn't slow down you are going to have a nervous breakdown?
- Do you need to have the sex talk with your child, but you don't know what is too much and what is enough?
- Do you need to potty train your child? Are you waiting for that perfect time?

Whatever your situation is, go ahead and do it! The longer you put off the inevitable, the worse it usually gets. Just think about how great you are going to feel when your junk drawer is clean. Imagine the relief when your credit card bill is zero! Think how encouraged you will feel when you AND your husband are tackling the situation with your teen together and you don't feel so alone. How relieved will you feel when you give the sex talk and it is not nearly as awkward or bad as you had imagined? Won't you LOVE not buying diapers? Whatever your obstacle is, overcome it and get it behind you!

REFLECTIONS

KEEP IT REAL

I just saw a television commercial that made me laugh. I don't know who writes these things, but they are SO unrealistic!

In the commercial, a mom is baking cookies and making icing with her children. They are all laughing and having a great time. At one point, the mom playfully puts icing on her little girl's nose. Of course the little girl laughs and smiles. They appear to be having the best day EVER!

That is not real life. REAL is not having the time to playfully bake cookies. REAL is baking "slice and bake" cookies and using icing out of a can. REAL is when you wipe icing on your child's nose and the child says, "Why did you do that?" REAL is just trying to keep your cool with your children in the kitchen. REAL is your child spilling their juice on the floor because they're inching closer to watch you slice the cookie dough. REAL is having to mop the floor while the cookies are baking. REAL is everyone finally enjoying a warm cookie and you feeling like an "okay" mom (not great, just okay). That is REAL!!!

I'm writing this to remind all of us that the commercial is NOT real! Life is not perfect and without mess. Keep it real! REAL is your child needing your daily love, attention, and boundaries much more than a "perfect" cookie moment. Besides, nobody wants icing on their nose . . . it just gets sticky!

Life is not perfect and without mess. keep it real!

REFLECTIONS

LESS IS MORE

Have you ever been to an amusement park or a football game and had an overwhelming feeling that you were being pushed from one area to the next? It almost feels like there is an invisible hand pushing you, and you are not controlling your destination. You are at the mercy of the crowd.

We can get the same feeling that we are in the "flow" of life, and we can't seem to break away from the culture or current we are in. It feels overwhelming at times. It seems to me that no matter what sport our child plays or what our interest is in life, society takes a good thing and injects some type of steroid into it until that weekend sport or activity turns into an all-consuming way of life. No longer is a baseball game just on Saturday mornings at the local ball field. No, in today's culture, it's an all-day event, traveling from county to county or state to state.

Gone are the days of a simple birthday party with cake and ice cream. That is an absurd thought in our society! No longer is it acceptable to have your child make his or her own Halloween costume the day of Halloween. These days elaborate costumes are bought and custom ordered months in advance.

What has happened to us? At some point in time, someone has to yell, "Stop pushing me!" It is okay to get off this crazy merry-go-round of life and bring back a simpler time when life moved at a slow pace, when families would sit on their front porches drinking tea and count the cars that went by. (I used to do this with my grandmother.) Sometimes in life less is more.

SOMETIMES IN LIFE, *less is more*

REFLECTIONS

LIFE IS NOT PASSING YOU BY

I was talking with my sweet Kelsey on the phone today, and Kelsey asked me what I was doing today. After I finished describing my plans, she was quiet. I knew exactly what she was thinking, because I've thought the same thing throughout my life as a mom. She was thinking, "That sounds like fun. What am I doing? Watching Evie and that's it."

I know how she feels. But let me stop and point out that raising a child is a job – a BIG job!!!! I honestly believe that the enemy whispers in our ear, "You are missing out! People will forget about you. You had talent and gifting once, but by the time you get back into the marketplace you won't have anything to offer."

I say, "That's a lie!" When you do reenter the market place, you will have a lot to offer because you will have learned skills you never had before: managing different personalities, finances, and temper tantrums; providing nutritional needs, fashion advice, transportation, and navigations skills; not to mention being a chef, counselor, administrator, and so much more I can't even type it all out! Ladies, when I went back to work, I was a better worker. I worked harder, was more creative, and was more productive. Don't underestimate your abilities. You are pouring all of your best into your child, and that is a wonderful thing.

Life is not passing you by. Trust me, life keeps going! I am 50 years old, and I feel like my career is just starting and the sky is the limit.

Raising a child is a job
— a BIG job!!!

REFLECTIONS

LOVE WITHOUT BOUNDARIES

"Neither height nor depth, nor anything else in all creation, will be able to separate us from the love of God that is in Christ Jesus our Lord." –Romans 8:39

God's love for us is unconditional. There is nothing that we can do that will ever separate us from His great love. Many times we believe that we have messed up to such a great extent and there is no way we could ever get back in His good graces. That is our human mind talking, and it is a lie. God's love for us does not have boundaries. Nothing and no one can separate us from God's love – not even ourselves.

As a mom, it is imperative that you believe those words and teach them to your children. We all mess up, we all sin, but God still loves us. God does not love conditionally – Praise God! God loves us despite our sinful ways. If you are a Christian, when God is looking at you, He does not see your sin, but sees His perfect, righteous Son, Jesus. Jesus paid the price of your sin, and your debt has been paid. When God looks at you, He sees Jesus and who you are because of Jesus.

The next time the enemy whispers in your ear that you are not good enough or worthy enough, or that your past is too great to forgive, shout at the top of your voice, "Get behind me Satan! God loves me! Neither height nor depth, nor anything else in all creation, will be able to separate me from the love of God!"

God's love
for us does NOT
have boundaries

REFLECTIONS

OBJECT OF OUR CONFIDENCE

I have learned over the years that there is only one person I can place all of my confidence, trust, and reliance in – God. I have been confident in my children's health, but then sickness happened. I have placed my confidence in myself, trying to operate a smooth household, and then chaos crept in. I have placed my confidence in Greg's job and salary, and then war broke out and he was recalled to active duty and had to leave his job at FedEx for deployment. Our first paycheck after he had left was $312! My point is, life happens. Things we think will never happen, do happen.

The question is, "Where do you place your confidence?" For me, the answer is God. God is trustworthy. God is reliable. All. The. Time. That is not to say that bad things will not happen. Many people think that if God is reliable, we will never suffer or have pain. But that is not even Scriptural! In the Bible, Jesus himself says in John 16:33, "In this world you will have trouble. But take heart! I have overcome the world." We will experience trouble, heartache, and death. If you are placing your confidence in never hurting, never being rejected, or not dying, your confidence will be shaken. But if your confidence is in God, you can have peace even when hard things happen.

This week, think about placing your confidence in God. He is a loving God who wants to be there for you always. He will walk through the difficult times with you. He has promised that he will never leave you nor forsake you. As a mom, you can have peace, knowing that no matter what comes your way, you have a loving Father walking with you every step of the way.

Where do you place *your confidence?*

REFLECTIONS

Patience is the one thing I have never totally gotten a handle on. I pray for it, I try with all my might to grasp it, but it is like cleaning up a broken egg on the floor – no matter how hard I try to grab it in one piece, I never can.

Why do we as moms pray for patience? Oh, I don't know, maybe because we NEED it! Ladies, from the time my children were babies, to now all grown up, I have needed patience every day. But, like I said, I have never mastered it. I would have occasional seasons where I was patient, but I never had patience 100 percent of the time. I would pray for patience first thing in the morning, and by 10am my patience would be gone.

If you are like me and patience eludes your grasp, let me leave you with a thought. Maybe we should change our focus from being patient in the moment to being patient overall. What I mean is that we should keep in mind that it takes at least 18 years for our children to mature and grow up (sometimes closer to 24 years). Our five-year-old is acting like a five-year-old because he is, in fact, five years old! Our teenager is acting immature because guess what, she is immature. If we keep in mind that this journey of motherhood takes time, we can be more patient with the process. We need to quit running it like it is a sprint, and start thinking of it as a marathon.

motherhood
IS A MARATHON

REFLECTIONS

PERMISSION TO BE HUMAN

Moms, how many times have you "messed up" in mommy world and then later kicked yourself for reacting the way you did or making a rash decision? How many times have you not believed your child's alibi and later found out they were telling the truth? When any of these situations happen (or a million different variations on those themes), we beat ourselves up. We don't let ourselves off the hook very easily, do we?

I cannot even count the number of times I have messed up as a mom. But we need to look at the bigger picture and realize that we are human! We WILL make mistakes. And that's okay. We tell our children, "It's okay, shake it off, you will do better next time" when they make mistakes. We need to take our own advice and apply it to motherhood. Shake it off, say you're sorry, forgive yourself, and move on!

This week, when you mess up (notice I didn't say IF, but WHEN, because you WILL mess up), give yourself some grace. Realize that your mistakes make you more lovable and approachable because "perfect" people are hard to be around. When you make mistakes, your children realize you are like them. It helps them relate to you.

Hang in there. We are all on a journey, and it's our first attempt at this motherhood thing, so we are learning as we go. I've been a mom for almost 26 years and I'm still learning AND still making mistakes! Let's give ourselves the same grace we give to our kids.

*When you **mess up** this week,*
*give yourself **some grace***

REFLECTIONS

Moms witness pity parties every week. When our children do not get their way, they pitch little fits of rage and then begin to feel sorry for themselves. Teenagers are the worst because they believe that the whole world is against them and they are the only ones who are suffering in such a horrible way.

We moms can put on a pretty good pity party too. Our husband goes on a work trip to another country: all expenses paid, first-class flight, five-star hotel, steak dinners, etc. Then we begin our pity party: we are stuck at home with the children, eating hot dogs and mac n' cheese again. We groan and complain that the never-ending job of a mom is way harder than we ever realized. We whine about how we never get a break. But, moms, don't stay in the pit of your pity party. It will only make you bitter and cold.

Many times hard and good run on parallel lines. We say to ourselves, "this is so hard!" but then we get to experience this deep love for our children and we say, "this is so good." Life is usually both. One reason being a parent is so rewarding is because you work hard at it and then you get to see your children bloom right in front of your eyes. There is nothing better!

Many times
HARD & GOOD
run on parallel lines.
Don't stay in the
PIT OF YOUR
PITY PARTY
in hard times.

REFLECTIONS

REMODELED LIFE

I recently remodeled our master bedroom. Unlike a TV show that dramatically unveils a beautiful house finished in an hour, my one bedroom took a lot longer than an hour. There was lots of planning, tearing out carpet, tearing down tile, covering up old paint with new paint, and taking down old window treatments. But as I waited for the process to be completed, I fell more and more in love with my bedroom.

I was thinking that the remodeling of my bedroom is a lot like the remodeling God does in my life as I walk with Him. I gave my heart to Jesus when I was seven years old. On that day, I became a new creation. Since then, God has taken the old Karen and started His remolding in my life: tearing down walls, ripping out false beliefs, and replacing them with His truth, which brings freedom and peace in Him. Every day God brings new things into my life, but in order for the new to look right and feel right, the old has to be taken down. Whether it is in my marriage or in motherhood, God gently shows me the things He is working on in my life. But it takes time. I am a work in progress.

I wonder where you are in the process? Are you just in the dreaming stage, wondering "what if" you invited God into your life, what would that look like? Or are you in the stage where you are ready to "remodel" and invite God in and say, "my life is Yours, do with me what You will." It is exciting and scary to totally trust in God to do whatever He wants with your life, but the end product is way more beautiful than you could ever imagine.

It is exciting and scary to totally trust God to do whatever He wants with your life, but the end product is *way more beautiful* than you could ever imagine.

REFLECTIONS

STRENGTH OF A LIFETIME

Have ever prayed and asked God for strength to be a good mom? I have, many times throughout my journey as a mom. I've prayed for strength when my children were younger and I wanted to laugh at their disobedience because they were so darn cute, but I knew I had to be strong so they would not repeat the behavior. Other times, I've prayed for strength when my child came to me crying because of hurt feelings from thoughtless friends or broken relationships. I've had to be strong and not allow myself to call the parent of the child and give them a few choice words.

Here is the truth: strength is built up over time. A non-runner can't instantly become a marathoner overnight. Training, work, pain, time, exhaustion, and feelings of defeat are all part of the process to gain enough strength to run a race. In order to become strong, we have to go through the hard stuff.

Life is just like training for a race. It's hard. But there is one key difference between training to run a road race and training to run the race of life: physical training is a choice, but we don't get to choose whether or not to train for the race of life. Like it or not, difficult times will come. And the struggles will stretch us. It is painful, but in the end the difficulties make us strong.

Moms, I get that this job is hard! It's honestly the hardest thing I've ever done, but I'm a better, stronger woman for being a mom, and for that I am very grateful!

STRENGTH
IS BUILT-UP OVER TIME

REFLECTIONS

THE HEART OF THE MATTER

"The heart is deceitful above all things and beyond cure. Who can understand it?"
–Jeremiah 17:9

Our emotions can rage war within us on a daily basis if we allow them to control us. One negative comment from someone, or a smirk on a family member's face, can make us believe people are angry at us, or cold-hearted, or even dislike us. The fact of the matter is, we do not know what people are thinking, and we should not allow our emotions to get the best of us. Emotions do not always represent truth.

If we believe the lie that our emotions represent truth, we could potentially destroy a friendship, or we could begin to build walls to protect ourselves from people. Walls only separate us and keep us isolated. In a mom's world, isolation is not a good thing. Instead of building walls, try renewing your mind. Tell yourself the truth: emotions do not always represent truth. Give your offender the benefit of the doubt. Try to believe the best in them and remind yourself that only God really knows the heart of another person.

Next time someone offends you, whether it be a family member or a stranger, try not to give in to your emotions and let them spin out of control. Instead, give your hurt to the Lord and ask Him to take your emotions and replace them with His love and compassion. You might be surprised at how seldom people will seem offensive to you with this new way of living.

REFLECTIONS

THE LOVE OF A MOM

I went to get my hair cut the other day. In the chair beside me was a mom with her eight-year-old son, who was playing video games. I heard the mom say to her stylist, "This is my son. He is autistic."

Instantly I had a new respect and admiration for this young mom. Her world on the outside looked exactly like mine – she was getting her hair done. But she's not just like me, because she deals with things with her son that I never have to think about. This sweet mom, like thousands of others just like her, carries a burden that a lot of us don't carry.

On the outside looking in, we are the same. But we are not the same. She has "extra" duties that I don't even consider. I would imagine every day brings new challenges, struggles, and tears. When she tries to teach her son a new concept, she has no idea if he is "getting" it or not. Stop for one millisecond and contemplate how hard that would be as a mom. She loves her child just as much as I love my son, Taylor, but her love has been stretched, challenged, and pressed to levels that I cannot even begin to comprehend.

Let's stop and raise a glass to moms who accept the challenges that come along with raising a special-needs child. At the end of the day, these moms love their children because they are wonderful, brilliant, loving, and most important, a special gift from God. These moms need to be praised!

REFLECTIONS

SPIRIT OF WISDOM

"I keep asking that the God of our Lord Jesus Christ, the glorious Father, may give you the Spirit of wisdom and revelation, so that you may know him better." –Ephesians 1:17

As I think back in my child-rearing days, one prayer got me through a lot of my days with small children when my husband traveled a lot. I would pray, "God, I KNOW You love me, that You will take care of me and provide for not just my spiritual needs, but also my relational needs and my physical needs. God, open up my eyes today so I will SEE You and not my circumstances, which I do not like."

I learned to depend on God for my physical needs because I could not depend on Greg when he wasn't home. I asked and prayed for relationships with friends, because I would get so lonely. God answered all my prayers.

Did God "fix" my issue by making Greg be home more? No, he did not.

Whatever situation you are in right now, I pray that God will "give you the Spirit of wisdom and revelation, so that you may know him better." The next verses say, "I pray also that the eyes of your heart maybe enlightened in order that you may know the hope to which he has called you, the riches of his glorious inheritance in his holy people, and his incomparably great power for us who believe."

I pray that God will open your heart to what He has called you to do, enable you to embrace your role 100 percent, and give you His wisdom in your life each and every day.

REFLECTIONS

THE WORTH OF A MOM

As I sit back and watch this next generation of women take on the huge task of motherhood, my heart is burdened for them. I am burdened because of the incredible pressure that our culture puts on moms. It seems to me that there is no longer a "voice of reason" speaking truth. Lies are spread until they sound like the truth. Moms are pressured to have picture-perfect lives, picture-perfect homes, picture-perfect children, and picture-perfect relationships with their husbands. It is ALL too much. Here is truth.

- First off, NOTHING in this world is perfect. You might need to write that down and place it all over your house.

- Second, our culture pushes us to have perfect home, decorated to magazine status, but that takes money – often money we don't have! Here is a little secret: Your children do not care. Children do not care how the home is decorated as long as mom is available for them. Children do not care where the sofa was purchased, or how much it cost, as long as mom will sit down on the sofa with them and read a book, watch a TV show, or play a game with them. Children do not care about things; what children care about is MOM.

- Third, the worth of mom is greater than rubies or diamonds. Our world doesn't teach that. Our world continues to pull moms in 500 directions, telling them that they have to do more and more until they are stretched too thin. The world says you can do it all and be successful, but I am here to tell you that you CANNOT do it all. Something will suffer.

Stay focused and stop comparing your life to magazines and other people. Cherish where you are.

REFLECTIONS

TO DREAM OR NOT TO DREAM

I am a dreamer. Dreaming about the future can be a great thing. The problem, however, is that with dreaming, expectations are sure to follow. And when expectations get into a situation, disappointment is close behind.

Keep God part of your dreams and you will not be disappointed, because you will not hold on to YOUR dreams too tightly. You will acknowledge, "God, these are my dreams, but what are yours?" That is having an open mind with your life. A closed mind is one that says, "this is my dream: I have to have two children, a boy and a girl, we must live in this part of town, earn this much salary, have a dog and a cat, and drive this car. My children will make all A's, my son will be the quarterback on the football team, and my daughter will be the cutest cheerleader." That type of thinking is a disastrous way to live. It will surely bring you and your loved ones frustration and turmoil. It is better to say, "These are my dreams, God. What are Your dreams for me? I submit to Your way. Less of me and more of You." Submitting your thoughts to God brings peace and love. Dream away! Don't be afraid to dream. But include God in ALL your dreams.

One last tip: If you are not a dreamer, but you are married to a dreamer, when your spouse dreams, say "Wow!" and not "How?" Most dreamers just want to talk about their dreams, but when they hear the word "How?", it frustrates them. This is a tip that Greg and I learned years ago, and it has really saved us from a lot of arguments!

KEEP GOD PART OF
your *dreams* and
you will not be disappointed

REFLECTIONS

ACTIONS SPEAK LOUDER THAN WORDS

What if you could never tell your child you love them – would they know and understand your love for them by your actions? How can you, as a parent, communicate your deep love to your child without saying the words "I love you?"

One great way to communicate love is to tell your child that he or she is uniquely and wonderfully made by God. Embrace the fact that your child is different and special in his own way. Communicate that you love his special qualities. Never expect him to perform like other children, but genuinely celebrate his own passions. A child is bound to feel loved when they are completely and wholly accepted.

Meeting your child's needs is another way to show love – not just her physical needs, but her emotional needs as well. Providing for a child's emotional needs does not always mean "fixing" their problems. Merely showing empathy, listening, helping them work through their emotions, and teaching them how to cope with their circumstances is a great way to show that you love them.

Perhaps the biggest way to show love to your child without ever saying "I love you" is to give your child your time. This gift is very hard to give, because these days our time is way more precious than words. In our busy lives as parents, it is easy to give a material gift to entertain our child. But what is more precious than sitting down with your child and spending some quality time with them? The busier you are, the more valuable your gift of time is to your child.

Be creative in the ways you speak and exhibit your love for your children. You may find truth in the old saying, "actions speak louder than words."

REFLECTIONS

BIRDS AND THE BEES

Many moms ask me when is the "right" time to talk to children about sex. Like everything else in parenting, there is no magic formula. I have four children, and I told them all at different times and in different ways. You, as a mom, have to adjust your talk according to your child's personality and temperament. Here are some overarching thoughts on the matter:

The sex talk cannot be just one talk anymore . . . it's a continual conversation. Start when they are very young, setting the foundation at 2–5 years old by teaching them not to allow anyone to touch their private parts. Continue to have conversations on this theme through high school.

Create a safe environment for your children to open up to you. Tell them that you are on their side. Be honest with them and encourage them to ask you questions instead of asking their friends, because you are experienced and you will tell them the truth.

Don't just say, "don't have sex," explain the why behind the no.

- For boys, talk about pornography and why it is harmful to their hearts and minds.
- For girls, explain to them that you understand the need to feel wanted and loved and you want that for them as well. Tell them that you want them to experience true love the way God designed it to be.

Talking about sex is awkward, but in our culture, peers, movies, and the media are leading too many children astray at every age. We as moms need to push aside our fear of awkwardness and instill wisdom into our children.

One last thing: keep in mind that your children may stumble and fall in this area. If or when that happens, you should be the first in line to show them unconditional love and compassion.

REFLECTIONS

BULLYING IS NO FUN FOR ANYONE

There is nothing more hurtful to a mom than to witness her child being made fun of by other children. Whether it is a playground incident, something that happened on the bus, or continued stories of how "mean" the girls are at your daughter's high school, bullying is real . . . and it is hurtful.

How does a mom navigate these waters? First off, try to keep in mind that children are still learning how to behave and how to have mature relationships with others. That doesn't make mean behavior okay, but at least it might help keep you from tearing the other child's hair out!

As a mom of four children, I dealt with these situations all the time. Sometimes it was my child who was not being kind to another child. Bottom line, bullying happens, so here's how I learned to deal with it:

- Empathy is powerful. Telling your child that you understand how the situation hurt their feelings, and that you understand why they were embarrassed, makes a child feel understood. Being understood is VERY important in building your influence with your child.
- Coach your child on how to respond to difficult situations. Keep in mind that your child may not know how to respond to a mean person. So many times we all get caught off guard when people are not nice to us. It will help your child know how to react better if you role-play situations with them: "If someone pushes you, how would you respond?" or "If someone calls you a name, should you fight back?"
- Teach your child to be kind. I used to tell my children that sometimes when a child is being mean to another child, it's because they are being hurt somewhere in their life.
- Remember how it feels. We can all find ourselves being treated unfairly, so teach your child to remember how it feels. Encourage them to be intentional in their own lives and not to treat others in an unkind way.

These tips may seem easy, but when you are dealing with feelings, friendships, and relationships, it is never easy.

REFLECTIONS

CONFIDENT CHILD

All parents want their children to be confident. I remember when Kelsey was three years old, SO full of confidence, a friend of mine asked me, "How did you instill such confidence in her?" I answered honestly, "I have no idea."

But now I have over 26 years of being a mom underneath my belt, and I believe I can answer that question with confidence. If you want confident children, allow them to do things on their own. I know what some of you are thinking that your child is shy. I understand that world too; Emily and Taylor were shy and did not ever want to push for their way.

Fast-forward to today: Emily is now a confident young woman, and Taylor is a man who continues to blow me out of the water with his transformation. He was my shyest child. When he was little, he refused to look people in the eyes because he didn't want to be noticed. I did not force him to be as outgoing as Kelsey, but I would encourage him to order his food at a restaurant or pick out his own clothes (even when they didn't match). As he grew, I encouraged Taylor to live a little outside his comfort zone. Each activity builds confidence in our children.

So many times we "do" for our children, telling ourselves we are helping them. But in reality we are not helping them, we are hurting them. If you want your child to be a confident adult, give them opportunities to stretch their wings and fly a bit. It takes time, and they will not get it on the first try, but before you know it, they will be soaring.

IF YOU WANT
confident children,
ALLOW THEM TO DO THINGS ON THEIR OWN.

REFLECTIONS

CUTTING THE APRON STRINGS

Many of you know that my youngest, Abby, just left for college in August. Greg and I are now empty nesters. Today's Tip on Motherhood is about how to cut the apron strings when your child goes to college.

Here are a few tips I've learned after moving four amazing kids into their dorm rooms for freshman year:

- Give your child some breathing room. College is about growing up. Sure, there is some real-world knowledge that has to be learned and experiences that must be had, but overall, college is a safe environment for a child to develop into an adult. It usually takes about four years. Give your child some space, and let him learn and grow on his own.
- Set your expectations early on so your child knows your rules. These are some of the rules that Greg and I set for our children:
    - Maintain your scholarship(s)
    - Graduate in four years
    - Spending money is your responsibility to earn or save
    - You may have a late curfew at school, but when you are home you are under our roof, and our rules apply
- When your children do come home, don't "fuss" at them. Try not to harp on them about how they never call, or never seem to care what you are doing. Let's be real here: when we were in college, did we think about our parents? Probably not.
- Send mail. College students love letters from home – yes, real snail mail letters. Care packages are great too. I was better at sending letters than packages, but I know my kids loved it when I made the effort to send a care package.
- Enjoy your young adult. Drink in your child when they visit. I love it when my college-age children come home! Their visits are usually short, but packed with intense hugs, conversations, and quality time.

The college years are great years! Enjoy them. For all the moms who are dreading this stage of life, I'm here to tell you, "it's not so bad!"

REFLECTIONS

DISCIPLINE IS HARD

When Taylor was in middle school, he would practice his golf chip shot in our front yard, hitting the ball toward the house. I asked him several times not to do that, and I told him that if he broke my double-pane window he would be paying to fix it. Well, you guessed it – he did not listen, and he broke the window. So Taylor had to cut grass all summer and earn enough money to pay us back for the broken window.

It was a LOT of work for me, too! But, I will tell you, it is our job as a mom to teach our child that we will follow through with the punishment. No one said it would be easy, no one said it would be pain-free. But if you are not going to take the time to teach your child how to live a responsible life, then who will?

A lot of times when you punish your child, it truly hurts you just as much as it hurts your child. But, moms, here is the thing: it is up to you to teach your child that their actions have consequences. As painful as it is for you as a mom, it is worth it in the long run. Taylor learned a great lesson that summer while he was cutting all of our neighbors' lawns, and while he was sweating and saving his money. He learned that his actions have consequences, and he also learned the value of money. It is hard to see these punishments through until the end, but you will be happy when you see the end result.

It is up to you to
TEACH YOUR CHILDREN
that their actions have
CONSEQUENCES.

REFLECTIONS

ENTITLEMENT

Our society breeds entitlement – the belief that one is deserving of certain privileges. Our children naturally think this way because when they are tiny, in many ways the world centers around them. As they get older, we can see that their self-centeredness is becoming problem, but we don't always know how to correct it.

Like anything, it is best to work on the problem before it becomes a problem. In other words, once your child gets to be three or four, start encouraging them to be more independent. Give them projects that they can do by themselves, such as:

- pick out their clothes for the day
- dress themselves
- help mommy put away the Tupperware from the dishwasher
- have them take their plate from the table to the sink

If you do everything for your child, your child becomes very dependent on you. They start to believe that they can't do anything right or perfect like you. After your child begins to feel inadequate, they then turn the corner to laziness. They develop the mindset, "why do I need to do it, when I know mom will do it better?" After that grows in them for a few years, your child is probably entering middle school and you have one entitled child on your hands. Not only is your child now entitled, they are in middle school and you are terrified to pull in the reins because you don't want them to rebel and go wild! As a mom, you are stuck . . . or so you think!

In reality, you are not stuck. You are STILL the mom, and you are the authority. It is just harder now. Don't wait too long, moms . . . train up your child in the way they should go. Don't wait until the teenage years, unless you love a challenge!

REFLECTIONS

FREEZE FRAME

There are times throughout our lives when we would just love to hit the pause button and freeze time. These are usually not the BIG moments of life you would think . . . your wedding day, the birth of your child, etc. No, for me they are more everyday type of shots, moments when everything feels as close to perfect as it can be. These are some of the times I've wanted to freeze:

- When Greg and I first started dating, one day in spring semester when he was driving me around the Georgia Tech campus showing me where his classes were and where he ate, lived, and walked.
- One summer night when the kids were five, three, and one, and everyone was ready for bed, and I put on music and the children danced around the room laughing, twirling, bouncing off of each other, and having the best time.
- A few years ago we went to Destin for a magical weeklong trip.

Recently, I experienced another freeze-frame time. I sat in a restaurant and watched all my children and their husbands sit and laugh and talk as adults. Greg leaned over and put his arm around my shoulder and said, "Are you okay? You are very quiet." I replied, "I am just soaking it all in." I was soaking in my freeze-frame moment.

Moms, our days are long and hard! Sometimes there is no rest for the weary and we just have to keep moving forward. But when God gives you one of those freeze-frame moments, stop and soak it all in. If you are not in a freeze-frame moment in life, remember back to when you were. It may be just the thing you need to get you through your day.

When God gives you a *"freeze-frame"* moment, stop and soak it all in.

REFLECTIONS

FULL HOUSE

"But in fact God has arranged the parts in the body, every one of them, just as he wanted them to be." *–1 Corinthians 12:18*

We think about our gifting and talents all the time, or at least I do. I am good at relationships, but I'm not great with administration stuff and I am horrible with numbers. Do you ever look at your children and think, "she is so talented in sports and music" or "he has such a creative eye for things?"

We've been talking about how our children are treasures and gifts from God. I think that even more as my children get older. And each one of them has a whole set of gifts and talents. Think about it this way: if you have two or three children, you probably have all kinds of gift sets right under your own roof. As a mom, you can take full advantage of that while they are in your home and allow God's body of Christ to work his full measure in your house.

Why should I go to a store and listen to a sales person trying to sell me an outfit when I have Kelsey? Who needs drugs to make me feel better when I have Emily around? Why should I pay someone to help me design an invitation when I have Taylor? Why do I need to pay a professional to come in and organize my house when Abby lives here full time?

When you ask your children their advice and their help, that instills in them the thought, "I matter to mom. She thinks I'm special and that I'm good at this."

REFLECTIONS

GET ON THE SAME PAGE - DISCIPLINE

How do you get on the same page as your spouse concerning discipline? Let's be honest: there are many times when we do not agree with our husbands. But when it comes to children, we MUST get on the same page! The reason we need to be "like-minded" is that children are smart. They learn from a very young age who is the more permissive parent and who is the stricter parent, and they will play one against the other. Always keep in mind that you and your spouse are a team. If the team is divided, you will not be effective.

That said, getting on the same page can be difficult at times. One parent is usually strict while the other parent is more permissive. Maybe your spouse was abused as a child, and they believe that if they discipline their child in any way, they will be abusing them. Does your spouse want to be your child's friend, and therefore doesn't want to be the parent? Or perhaps your spouse is a "Type A, need for control" type of person, and discipline takes precedence over all else, making your home feel like the army.

I think one of the best ways to get on the same page as your husband is to look around and find a family that has teenagers who turned out great. Invite those parents out to dinner and ask them how they disciplined their children. Take notes.

After the dinner, go home and discuss with your spouse the best takeaways from what you learned and how you can start applying them to your family. You may need to have several conversations at different times, but at least you are moving in the right direction. And more importantly, you are moving together.

Always keep in mind that you and your spouse are
A TEAM

REFLECTIONS

HARD WORK

How often do you sit down with your child and just enjoy them as a person? Not correcting them, not giving motherly advice or saying, "sit up straight and don't chew with your mouth open" or "stop biting your nails, stop making that annoying noise, and stop shaking your leg non-stop." Honestly, as moms, we are always "on" and "working." Rarely do we just enjoy our child for who they are – enjoy the silliness, the quirky smiles, and their love of life.

It's important to work on our relationships with our children. We need to carve out time and energy to get to know each child as an individual person, separate from us. This philosophy especially applies as our children get older and start to develop a personality of their own, with thoughts and ideas of their own. So many times as a mom I push against any new idea my child has because it is different from mine. But if I want a relationship with my children, I need to work at it. I need to stop and listen to what my child is saying. Quite often I discover that their idea is good – it might be different from mine, but it is good and it is theirs. Sometimes I need to push past what annoys me about my child and find something that I love about them to focus on.

Our children need us to be their advocate and for us to fight for our relationship with them, even when it's hard. This is especially challenging when they transition from child to adult. Nothing in life comes easy, and your relationship with your children is no different. But keep on fighting for them. You will one day be so glad you did.

REFLECTIONS

LEAD BY EXAMPLE

Moms are always asking me the best way to teach their children to follow after God's heart.

I believe that the best way to teach children – or anyone, for that matter – is to lead by example. As moms we should always ask ourselves the question, "Do my actions line up with my words?"

- If you want your child to love well, then you need to love well.
- If you want your child to have a generous heart and be compassionate toward others, then you need to serve others and love them even during the rough times.
- If you want your child to be honest, then you need to be honest in every aspect of your life.
- If you want your child to be walking with the Lord on a daily basis, then you need to be walking with the Lord and learning from him each day.

I shouldn't be asking my children to do anything that I am not already doing myself. God needs to be a priority in my life if I want Him to be a priority in my child's life.

Don't make the mistake of believing that your children are not paying attention – they are. Children are always watching you. They are noticing how you treat others in the grocery store, the mall, or in traffic. They are taking notes, whether you see it or not. Is your life worth taking notes on? I know that is a tough question . . . but it's one that you should ask often.

REFLECTIONS

LOVE BEYOND LIMITS

Moms are "fixers." We fix broken toys, torn shirts, stained pants, and sick children. When our children are hurt emotionally by a friend or loved one, we try to fix those situations as well. But we cannot always fix things. Sometimes our best efforts only seem to make the situation worse.

What is a mom to do? We can have empathy and listen to our children's broken heart, but acknowledge, "mom cannot fix this for you, but God can." Many times as a mom, we need to point our children to God and teach them to take their hurt and their anger to God and leave it in His very capable hands.

To point your child to God is to acknowledge that you are in fact human, but you love and serve an almighty God who is not human – who is a powerful, holy, sovereign God. A God who wants to hear your child's hurt, to take on their burdens, and who is on their side. The gift that you will be giving your child is immeasurable. You may not be able to always fix things, you may not even be around physically to help your child, so point them to God, who will always be there to guide and direct them in all things.

You may not always be able
to fix things for your child,
POINT THEM TO GOD,
who will always be there to
guide and direct them
in all things.

REFLECTIONS

NEVER SETTLE

One of the biggest challenges I face as a mom is when my child and I are not getting along. This battle takes on many forms. It happened when my child was two and was throwing temper tantrums, when my child was 10 and was not doing their best in school, when my child started rolling his/her eyes at me, or even in the teen years, when every conversation ended in an explosion. Whatever the age, it is not fun, and it's easy to feel very defeated as a mom. There is also a little voice in the back of my brain telling me, "You just can't get along with this child. You might as well give up, it's impossible."

Moms, I'm writing today to tell you to NEVER settle for a less-than-great relationship with your child. Yes, sometimes we as moms must keep moving forward, even when it feels like the current of resistance is so strong that it threatens to sweep us away . . . but don't settle. Whatever you need to do to build a relationship with your child, keep doing it.

That does not mean, however, that you need to allow your child to keep pitching fits, not do their homework, explode all over you, or treat you like a doormat. Keep working on the relationship. Keep fighting to motivate your child, understand your child, and parent your child.

Moms, don't settle. Keep fighting for your child, and don't ever give up on the relationship. It's worth it in the long run.

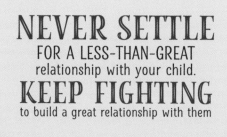

NEVER SETTLE
FOR A LESS-THAN-GREAT
relationship with your child.
KEEP FIGHTING
to build a great relationship with them

REFLECTIONS

RAISING BOYS

Allow Boys to be Boys

I think it is really important for moms to allow their boys to be boys. Taylor scared me to death with all of his climbing and getting into things, but Greg told me from the beginning to let him be a boy.

Be a Protector

We have to teach our sons how to protect ladies and stand up for them. This lesson starts when they are young. In practical terms, this may mean teaching your son to hold the door open for his sisters and allow them to go first. Boys need to learn that it is NEVER okay to hit a girl, even when they make him mad. It is also important to teach them that girls don't want to hear about farts and burps.

Teach Them How to Love

In the Bible, men are instructed to love their wives and wives are told to respect their husbands. A mom can start teaching her son how to love a woman long before he is old enough to marry. Teach your son to put others before himself. Teach him to treat a girl respectfully, like a lady, and never degrade her.

Teach Responsibility

One of the most important things I believe Greg and I did in raising Taylor was to teach him responsibility. Even as a young boy, Taylor would help Greg around the yard. As he grew older, we encouraged him to get a job – any job – so he could learn the value of money.

REFLECTIONS

RAISING GIRLS

It is so important to tell a little girl she is beautiful and talented on a regular basis. But it is even more important for a girl to learn what true beauty is. True beauty comes from the heart. My mom used to tell me when I was growing up, "Pretty is as pretty does," meaning that if you are pretty on the outside, but not pretty on the inside, then you lose your attractiveness. When you see your daughter being kind, praise her. I believe we should praise a person's good actions more than their outer appearance.

Accept your daughter for the way she is. Don't try to change your little girl to make her someone she is not. Learn to celebrate her for the way God created her. She will be a more confident girl and woman if she grows up being herself. In a society where everyone tries to be the same, show her how important it is to celebrate being who you are, and that you should not change to fit into someone else's mold.

You have something in common with your daughter; you are both women, complex and beautiful creatures. Sometimes as a mom the best thing you can do is put your arm around your girl and say, "I understand."

- I understand you are scared
- I understand you want to be her friend
- I understand your feelings are hurt
- I understand your hormones are driving you crazy
- I understand your heart has been broken
- I understand . . .

Those are reassuring words to a young girl who doesn't understand why life is so cruel at times. A mother's arms and those two words can make things a little – and sometimes a lot – better.

REFLECTIONS

◦ TOUGH YEARS ◦

So many times we focus totally on our child's behavior, and we forget to take a look into what is going on in their little lives. We dismiss their problems instead of taking them seriously. My challenge to you this week is to take some time to examine what's going on in your child's world, especially when your child acts out, has a change in personality, or is just not acting like himself.

I can remember vividly when I was in sixth grade and my BEST friend for over a year was placed in a different classroom from me. Even though our classes were right next to each other, it felt like we were miles apart. To make matters worse, she had one of the coolest girls in our school in her new class. You guessed it – they instantly became BEST friends. All of a sudden my best friend was not calling me and did not play with me on the playground. To make matters worse, she shared all her secrets with this new best friend. I was left standing on the outside looking in. All of a sudden, I was not cool, not in the "In" crowd, and it rocked my world.

Moms, there is a lot that goes on in your child's world between 7:30 in the morning and 3:00 in the afternoon. If you want influence with your child, don't dismiss their "problems" and act like they are no big deal, because to a child they are a huge deal. We as moms need to have empathy, offer a compassionate ear, and always give love. We may not be able to shield our children from life (nor should we even try), but we can provide a safe, warm, loving home to retreat to each day.

REFLECTIONS

TRUST YOUR MOM INSTINCTS

I'm realizing that all moms are alike. We all seem to struggle with the same type of problems. One struggle I see more and more is that moms lack confidence in their parenting style. I'm not sure the reason behind this damaging trend. I don't know if it is a spiritual matter, or if these moms just feel like they are the only fish swimming in the right direction. It seems that the more traditional moms end up feeling like freaks of nature!

I'm here today to give you a little pep talk. You are not a freak of nature! You are wise beyond your years, and God has given you the important job of raising the next generation, so stand firm in your thinking. You are not your child's friend until they are self-sufficient and living on their own. Trust in your gut and your God-given instincts, even if other parents do not agree with you.

So many moms say to me, "What if I am the only mom who doesn't allow my child to play video games all day?" or "What if I'm the only mom who doesn't let my child get a cell phone in 2nd grade?" or "What if I am the only mom who doesn't drop off my middle schooler at a local shopping area to roam around for four hours with other tweens with no chaperone?" or "What if I am the only mom who doesn't allow my child to talk disrespectfully to me?" My response: "Good for you! Your child will thank you one day."

Trust your instincts as a mom, and if you don't know what to do, ask God to give you wisdom.

Trust in your gut & your
God-given instincts

REFLECTIONS

TURN IT OFF

Our children are becoming addicted to technology. Actually, we as moms are addicted too, if we are honest with ourselves. How many times do I check email, Twitter, and Facebook on my phone throughout the day? Recently I've even gotten addicted to playing solitaire on my phone. It's true! I play it all the time, and I can't stop until I win. Our children are the same way . . . just because a game is "educational" doesn't mean it isn't addicting for them. So my tip for the week, or should I say my challenge for the week, is to turn off the technology and send your children outside to play.

When my children were young, I would turn off the television, send them outside to our fenced-in backyard, and lock the back door so they could not come back inside. I would tell them to get out in the yard and use their imaginations. Of course, my children are just like yours, and they would fuss and whine and ask to come back inside. I would stand inside and say, "No, you go play. You can come in at lunchtime." I know, many of you are gasping right now, thinking, "How could Karen be so cruel?" But, let me put your minds at ease: my children did not die! Quite the opposite, they ended up having a great time! Usually by lunchtime they were so far gone into their imaginations that I would have to beg them to take a break and come in for lunch.

If you don't want robots for children, you must turn off the electronics. Take away their iPads and cell phones and teach them how to play with each other and how to have fun using their God-given imaginations.

**turn off the technology
and send your children
*outside to play***

REFLECTIONS